The Seris

DAVID L. BURCKHALTER

The University of Arizona Press
Tucson, Arizona

About the Photographer...

DAVID L. BURCKHALTER, a self-trained photographer, developed his talent during several years of regular trading and photographing trips to the land of the Seris. He has also photographed in the western United States, central Mexico and in Afghanistan and India. He holds degrees from the University of Arizona, and the University of Kansas. As of 1976, he was working in Tucson, Arizona teaching and freelancing.

Second Printing 1978

THE UNIVERSITY OF ARIZONA PRESS

I.S.B.N. 0-8165-0517-9
L. C. No. 75-44915

Behind the Lens

My first awareness of the Seris came in 1968 after meeting a group selling crafts outside a restaurant by Kino Bay. I enjoyed bargaining with these people and made a purchase. I returned, and by late 1969 was involved in the woodcarving trade. The Seris, however, had much more to offer than their crafts. The people and their special ways were of great personal interest to me, and my visits to Seriland increased.

The day's activity in a Seri village begins when dawn camp fires are lit to prepare the morning meals. The fishermen leave in their boats. Children are up and about performing their chores. Many adults are idle, enjoying the morning stillness. The ever present smells of ironwood smoke and the salt sea drift and mingle with the breeze. A quiet day proceeds, broken perhaps by a dogfight or an airplane passing overhead. A family—loaded into their pick-up truck—is off to Kino Bay looking for tourist customers. Throughout the village is heard the hacking and filing of artisans carving ironwood. Others may be making baskets or stringing necklaces. Activity increases as boats return with fish and turtles, and excited groups gather to view the catch. At the store some people are meeting and exchanging gossip. The craft buyer or stranger, just arrived in town, finds the mood relaxed and friendly. Stopping in at one of the stores to quench his thirst after a hot and dusty trip, the traveler usually is met on the way out by a group—mostly women and children—adding last-minute polishes to woodcarvings and dangling shell necklaces for sale. Greetings come in the Seri language, Spanish, or even English. The quality, quantity, and variety of the crafts combined with good humored bargaining enliven the encounter and sales are readily accomplished. With formalities over, there are rounds to make and special friends to visit. The boats are in, business is concluded, and evening brings families together to eat and relax. Children play while fish and tortillas are cooked for the late meals. There are moments to talk and reflect the events of the day. As fires and lanterns fade, a clear starry night creeps over the village and the sea, and one experiences a feeling of timelessness.

In my visits to Seriland over the past five years, I have attempted to capture on film the uniqueness of the Seris. The village of Desemboque appealed to me because of its isolation, tranquility, and contrast. "Desemboque" means, and was for me, "a disembarking place."

I am indebted to David Coffas and Edward H. Spicer for their help in preparing this book. I also thank the University of Arizona Press for publishing my work.

David Burckhalter

Capturing the Feeling

EDWARD H. SPICER

We take away from this portfolio a memory of faces. The people look towards us deeply from within. The strong, level gazes hold us with their sudden presence. The people of the faces we see seem to be saying: "We are Seris, looking out at you from our own unique experience as a people. We do not forget that experience and we measure you in its light."

One wonders how the photographer has eliminated himself from each situation and captured the essence of these people. Never do we see smiling self-consciousness— nearly always we seem to be conducted to the very threshold of the Seri spirit. Maria Luisa's seamed face dominating the beach scene behind her, the three generations of women's faces at Rosita Mendez's household, the strong, penetrating gaze of Pancho Hoeffer, the "conservative"—these portraits and many others testify to the photographer's talent for bringing us to each individual on that person's own terms, so that he or she remains in our memory as unforgettably unique.

It is not the faces alone that constitute the photographer's great accomplishment. He has managed something akin to what was done in the great portraits by painters of the Renaissance. He has brought together people and settings in a way that deepens the sense of who the persons are. Like the Renaissance painters, he gives us bits of landscape and seascape and selected pieces of the man-made world glimpsed in backgrounds beyond or surrounding the person. The primary focus is on the faces, but their world, cultural and natural, makes a simultaneous impression—the woman's face, with the boat being pulled up on the beach far beyond, the shining evening wavelets like scales overlapping one another, the giant cactus in discrete profusion in the far background. To be sure, it is not the whole world of the Seri people. There is no pretense at giving us a whole ethnography, a catalog of the cultural environment. Rather, the selected elements, as in the Renaissance portraits, suggest the whole world of the period in which the people live. The portraits and remarkable pictures of the desert shore and the conglomerate fishing village of Desemboque make it very clear that these are people who live at the edge of the gulf waters between the desert and the sea. They are people living on and with the sand. There is no mistaking that these people are deeply and constantly at home with the sand, and the sea, and the desert.

It is also clear, as we note these excerpts from the natural and the cultural world of the Seris, that the man-made part of it consists of things which Seris do not make themselves. A home is a shelter of manufactured corrugated tarpaper nailed to poles to make a sun-screen over the sand for a living room and for a windbreak as in the once used ocotillo frame shelters. All around are big oil drums for water storage and a dozen other uses. The living space under the tarpaper is furnished with enamelware coffeepots and cups, tin pans, and lengths of car-springs and cut tops of cans for cooking over the open fires. Everything for eating, for cooking, for sewing, for carving is spread out on the sand while the people are doing things, then it all is piled up together when the Seris are loafing and joking under the sun-screens. Home life is on the sand in intimacy with the beach, but is also with things of the machine age.

Everywhere are the signs of continuing invasion from the outside world. The women, looking for opportunities to trade, gather about a car that has driven in from Michigan. The stores are run by Mexicans, not by Seris. The silhouetted outlines of the outboard motors (encouraged by the Mexican fish buyers) on the ends of the boats become a symbol of the ongoing commercial invasion. A lovely polished fish carved of iron-wood is lost in the miscellany of enamelware and metal things in a household scene, non-functional there but ready for sale in the art goods market in cities of the United States and Mexico. We see the white woven palm hats which Mexican manufacturers have managed to spread all over Mexico. There is a jumble of cultural traditions, but each element is selected and adapted by Seris to their needs. What appears to the outsider as a clutter is not that in Seri life, but a selection of the most useful things from the mixed bag that modern life offers.

The photographer does not grope through the haze of romantic yearning and misconception which so often distorts the interpretation of Indian life. Here he has caught the Seris in one of the five crucial moments in their history. This is the moment of the revival of their seacoast life after facing extinction barely thirty years ago. They are caught in these pictures living the life to which they have won their way back after 300 years of fighting off attempts by Spaniards and Mexicans to change them into a wholly different kind of people.

The glimpses of the settings for the portraits open vistas into the history of the Seris as a people. The present phase in much of its complexity is firmly there in the photographs, but for fuller understanding of the people who confront us, we need to be aware of the experiences they have survived during the last three centuries. The present phase constitutes a special triumph. In the early 1900s, after centuries of effort, the last of a succession of invaders gave up trying to drag the Seris away from their beloved seacoast. The Seris, after all, seemed obviously on the way to final extinction. There were little more than 100 left of the thousands who had made the gulf coast their home when Spaniards first encountered them in the late 1600s. It was hardly worth it for the Mexican ranchers to go on forcing them into the haciendas and big ranches as laborers, and the Sonoran government had long since given up in its attempts to make farmers out of fishermen. The few remaining Seri families were at last left to themselves to die out in their own way.

But, instead, from the 1920s to the present the Seris began a series of adaptations which constitutes an amazing comeback from extinction. This has been accomplished by bringing the resources of their desert-seacoast habitat into a working relationship with the economic realities of Mexico and the United States. The great demand for shark livers by the immensely expanding world market for vitamins during the 1930s gave Seris their first strong foothold in the modern world. They learned the technology of the plank boat and fished for sharks. Here and there on the beaches one can still see the piles of gray sun-toughened shark skins marking the places where Seris disembowelled the catches and gathered the livers for the distant market. It was a decade before synthetics replaced shark liver for vitamins, but in that time Seris were launched on a new way of life in their chosen homeland.

As the shark liver market slumped forever, Seris found themselves able to move easily into seafood production for the faraway markets of the Sonora, Arizona, and California cities. They now knew how to build plank boats and use the fishing gear to which Mexican fishermen had introduced them. Now the Mexican fish buyers coming to the coast rented and sold them outboard motors. Their fishing technology was enriched again and Seris during the next 25 years became entirely enmeshed in a cash economy. They caught and sold sea bass and red snapper and sea turtles to the Mexican fish buyers who sold them in the inland cities. Seri population began to increase in the 1950s and then steadily continued its growth. This second adaptation seemed solidly based. They had demonstrated even to the Mexican government—which had always regarded Seri life as something that needed to be changed—that the Seris' way could work. Government advisers stepped in twice to help by organizing fishing cooperatives. Twice these outside-inspired efforts failed, until finally the Seris again were left alone to solve their own problems.

By the late 1950s the market for fish fell off and the turtles became more scarce. The Seris during the 1940s already had begun to be known for their well-made baskets in the same cities where their sea produce was sold. Basket buyers, as well as fish buyers, came to the Seri camps along the coast and bought baskets from the women basketmakers as the men sold their fish and turtle meat. Now the craft trade sought another Seri product, namely, carefully carved and polished sculptures of wood which a few Seri men began to make. Steadily, demand for these objects increased through the 1960s. The reddish-brown ironwood of the surrounding desert provided the material. Using whatever metal tools, such as files and saws, they could get, men began to carve more and more fish, turtles, seahorses, quail, sharks and other sea and desert forms. By the 1970s woodcarving had begun to supersede fishing in importance, and Seris were linked in another way with the market economy of the world.

It is in this moment of history that the photographer has etched a record of the Seri spirit in their own setting. For Seris have chosen in the face of almost overwhelming odds to return to the seacoast and to make their way there as the clutter of twentieth-century life intrudes on them. They have found successive ways to adapt to this life, using its own ways of technology and commerce. They have demonstrated that they could do so, once the restraints and interferences of the Spaniards and the Mexicans were fended off. The photographs of this volume express the Seri triumph.

The Seri historical experience is worth considering, by way of deeper appreciation of the position of insight to which the photographer has brought us. Jesuit missionaries, Spanish and German, never learned the Seri language but worked tirelessly at conversion beginning in 1679. During some 80 years they walked the desert lands of western Sonora trying to persuade the 4,000 or more Seris to settle at missions which they established inland, chiefly along the San Miguel River in the vicinity of what is now Horcasitas. The Jesuits had a vision—never to be realized—of leading all the Seris from what the missionaries regarded as uninhabitable coast to irrigated farmlands of the central valleys. The road to civilization, they were convinced, lay through residence in farming villages. Nearly 1,000 Series responded to the indefatigable labors of the missionaries and took up residence at one or more of the new mission towns, but they came and went and seemed disinclined to settle down permanently. However, after nearly a century, more than 800 Seris had decided to settle down, chiefly at a place called Los Angeles on the San Miguel River. Then, in the midst of what seemed a growing success in the missionary efforts, Spanish soldiers moved in and appropriated the lands prepared for the Seris. The Seris protested, as did the missionaries, but found the Spaniards ruthlessly determined to uproot Indian families. All the women of the Seri colonists were rounded up and deported southward, probably to Guatemala. This ended all voluntary acceptance by Seris of the new way of life. Bitterly, they left the missions and began what they must have regarded as a truly just war against the Spaniards who had destroyed their families. The doublecross by the Spanish soldiers and civil authorities was effective in turning Seris forever against the Jesuit program for "civilization."

The Seri men who had tried farming and lost their families left the mission world of the San Miguel, and joined the great majority of Seris who never had been converted by the Jesuits. Together they sought to drive the Spaniards out of the whole area around what is now Hermosillo. This was the farthest thrust up to then by the invaders towards the country in which the Seris lived. The next 30 years would undoubtedly be remembered by Seris, if they had had means of keeping the record, as one of the greatest moments in their history. They maintained a stronghold in the Cerro Prieto south of Pitic (later Hermosillo) from which they continually attacked the Spanish settlements to the north. The Spaniards seemed unable to gain any military successes for more than a decade. In one defensive battle, the Seris killed a governor of Sonora. Two Seri military leaders became famous among Spaniards under the names of "Becerro" and "Boquinete," and it was reported that Seris were able to put 400 fighting men into the field. This must have meant that there were as many as 3,000–4,000 Seris banded together in this great resistance to further encroachment by the untrustworthy Spaniards. It was a phase of Seri history during which deep and lasting hatred and hostility to the representatives of civilization grew strong. The hostility was so great that the first Franciscan missionary to try to work with the Seris was killed and the beginnings of a mission building within Seri coastal territory destroyed. But Seris simply were not powerful enough to withstand the growing number of Spanish soldiers. By the 1780s Seri unity began to crumble under renewed pressures, and family groups, one by one, came down out of the black hills to surrender. They were seeking food. By 1790 Seri resistance in the Cerro Prieto was wholly broken, and only isolated bands were left roaming the coast.

With Seri resistance broken, the Spaniards began a new series of attempts, later carried further by the Mexicans, to force Seris into the settled, farming life. They chose a site on the Sonora River across from the growing town of Pitic. The new site was called Villa de Seris. Irrigation canals were constructed and fields were laid out. As Seri families came out of the hills to surrender, they were settled at the new community and began to farm. The various Seri bands probably by this time had been reduced to no more than 1,500 individuals—less than half the original population. The Seris who were forced after surrender to settle at Villa de Seris found it impossible to adapt to the hostile and domineering behavior of their Spanish neighbors. Again, one by one, the families quietly left and went out into the coastland to live as best they could. The Spaniards were not much concerned. Many wanted the developed land, and as each family left, Spaniards took over the fields. By 1793 there were no more Seris at Villa de Seris, except for those children the Spaniards had adopted forcibly. However, during the course of nearly a century, the attempts to resettle the Seris were continued sporadically, by means of extreme force. In 1807 Spaniards made the first raid into the Seri heartland on Tiburón Island, rounded up Seri families, and brought them again to Villa de Seris. As these Seris died or drifted away new roundups were made, one of the largest taking place in 1844 when 500 Seris were captured alive and brought to Hermosillo. By 1880 there were 150 Seris living unhappily at Villa de Seris, but in that year they found ways to flee after Mexicans attempted to kill them by poisoning their flour. The government efforts to resettle the Seris ended, as complete a failure as the missionary attempts to do the same thing 150 years before. It seems likely that by about 1880 there were no more than 500 Seris left of the original 4,000 or more, and the legacy of mutual hatred from Spanish times was even stronger.

For the next 40 years—from about 1880 until about 1920—the encounters between Seris and Mexicans took place within the Seris' own territory. The use of windmills to pump water from wells at the edge of the rainless coastal margins made it possible for Mexican cattlemen to expand westward from central Sonora towards the coast. The few remaining Seris found themselves fighting desperately for their very existence within their old homeland. Hostilities grew intense as Seris killed an occasional beef, and cowboys retaliated ruthlessly. The new invaders believed wholeheartedly in the complete and utter savagery of the Seris and considered them non-human. One rancher, however, established at a ranch called Costa Rica within the Seri homeland, felt that he might save the Seris from extinction. He selected two Seri youths to be specially educated, hoping to train them so they could become a bridge to civilization for the Seris. The plan failed. One youth abandoned Seri life entirely and the other was reabsorbed among the Seris. Sporadic warfare between cowboys and Seris went on into the twentieth century, and Seris moved closer and closer to extinction as their numbers fell to less than 200. The third attempt to change the Seri way of life—by "education"—had failed as had the two previous efforts.

The tide turned during the 1920s and early 1930s when the present moment of Seri history began with new adaptations based on the Seri choice to maintain themselves in their seacoast homeland. This is a period of triumph. Seris have prevailed against successive efforts to force them into a mold not of their choosing. It is also a precarious moment in Seri life. They have made successful use of the commercial system of Western civilization. They have survived and begun to increase again in number. They even have impressed their art forms on the dominant society. But, they also are subject to myriad forces of modern civilization which could lead to the disintegration of the distinctive Seri patterns of living. They are vulnerable through schools whose teachings ignore the values of the life adapted to the desert and the sea. They are vulnerable through religious proselytization by missionaries who, like the Jesuits, focus on change without reference to traditional values. They are vulnerable to the scramble for economic advantage and the other commercial values that impinge on them daily. The recent return to the Seris by the Mexican government of one of their heartland areas—Tiburón Island—may signal better understanding of Seri interests by the dominant society, but governments in Seri experience have always been helpful only on the governments' terms.

The photographs in this book bring us to the threshold of understanding the identity of a people who have weathered devastating storms of history. They bring us into contact with the spirit of a people. The photographs spring from deep respect for and sensitivity to the Seri spirit in its present moment—carrying its special qualities from a harsh and sometimes heroic past through a precarious present into an unknown future.

We are Seris

looking out at you from our own unique experience as a people.
We do not forget that experience, and we measure you in its light....

Seri conservative and his daughters...*Pancho Hoeffer.*

Matron of the Burgos family…*María Sara.*

Seri matron and young girl...*Sara* and *Marta*
...Sara is one of the first-encountered and
ever-present personalities of Desemboque.
She has no family, and makes her living
by selling her necklaces, dolls, and baskets
to tourists. Marta is often seen as
her companion.

Seri matron...*Augustina Burgos.*

Seri portrait...*Pedro Comito.*

Seri portrait...*Francisca* and daughter.

A Seri woodcarver and shaman
...*Fernando Romero.*

Seri portrait...A young girl...A family rich in daughters is rich in possessions. A bride price of a boat, a motor, some livestock, or money is the Seri custom.

Old woman with a file...*María Luz.*

Sara in the desert with her walking stick and cup.

There is
no mistaking

that these people are deeply and constantly at home
with the sand, and the sea, and the desert....

Seriland...Cardon cactus forest...The Seris have lived for centuries in this desert environment.

Desemboque seascape…Looking South from Desemboque. Tepopa Point is prominent, and beyond are Tiburón Island and the Sea of Cortez.

Desemboque, Sonora, Mexico...This village was established as a fishing center in
1942 by Seris who moved here from Tiburón Island and Kino Bay.

The catch...A group of Seris cleaning fish.

Distributing the catch...A common occasion for a break in the day—a fishing boat comes in.

Desemboque...The main thoroughfare...Varying numbers of Seris—seldom more than two hundred—live here throughout the year. The people have no modern facilities, and they have limited contact with the outside world.

Late afternoon street scene, Desemboque…Street life varies from
near desertion to bustling activity toward the end of the day.

Seri gathering...*María Sara's* family...Resting in the afternoon shade of her prosperous son's house, María displays the basket she is making.

Angelita's kitchen.

Beachscape...*María Luisa* and fishermen.

Old man at home...*Antonio Burgos.*

Freshly washed utensils...
Lupe Comito and child.

Afternoon walk along the Desemboque beach.

Nightfall…Sometimes, at this time of day, singing may be heard in the village.

Everywhere are the signs

of continuing invasion from the outside world....

At Teniente's store...The few general stores of Desemboque are Mexican owned and operated.

Cadillac from Michigan…Waiting with wrapped carvings for the gringos to return to their car, these women are dressed in the typical Seri style, adapted from turn-of-the-19th-century outside influences.

In front of Oscar's store...
Lola Blanco and her wares.

Three Seris...*Nacho, Fernando,* and *María Luisa*...Nacho's tied hair and kilt are a conservative contrast to Fernando's Mexican appearance. María Luisa is the eldest of the Seri matrons.

Seri dandy…A young man…Most young Seri men have adopted Mexican fashions. Cowboy hats, boots, and western shirts are worn in individual combinations. Many young men seem to disregard the old ways.

Seri badge and gun...*Roberto Herrera*...Roberto, the Desemboque constable, displays a humorous quick-draw tactic that he sometimes uses on gringos and Mexicans. He also is known for his knowledge of Seri history, language, and customs.

Punta Chueca shoreline…Looking toward Tiburón Island. Seri-made boats fit the seascape.

There is a jumble

of cultural traditions, but each element is selected
and adapted by the Seris to their needs....

Portrait of Eva's daughter.

Summer ramada…A traditional ocotillo frame shelter stands temporarily vacant in Punta Chueca.

Seris enjoy a good joke...*Pancho Molino's family.*

A family spread…The tarpaper house, open ramada, and scattered possessions are common sights in Seriland.

A woodcarving family...*Ramón Perales* at work.

Seri interior...*María Luz Díaz* at home...María Luz displays a carved fish for sale.

Woman siphoning water from a drum...
María Antonia... Fresh water, always a
major concern of Seri survival, is available
from village wells and stored in drums
for community use. *María Antonia*, like
other Seri women, wears a collection of safety
pins—readily available for a variety of uses.

Playing the one-stringed violin for his own enjoyment...*Jesús Morales.*

The cigarette portrait...*Sara*
...Sara is one of the few Seris
who smokes cigarettes.

Afternoon...*María Luisa* visiting the Mexican nurse.

The stranger

just arrived in town, finds the people friendly....

Three generations of Seri women...*Rosita Méndez* and her younger relatives.

School beginners...Desemboque school has been open since the early 1950s.

The grin…A Desemboque youngster.

Seri sisters.

A painted face...*Eva*...Face painting, no longer a common sight, once was practiced daily. Now it is seen only on special occasions.

We seem to be

conducted to the very threshold of the Seri spirit....

Seri portrait...*Pancho Hoeffer.*

Seri portrait...*Jesús Ibarra.*

Seri portrait...*Angelita Torres* wearing a blouse with distinctive Seri piping.

Blind woodcarver...*Alberto Villalobos.*

Blind woodcarver's wife…*María Luz.*

Seri classic...*Sara Villalobos.*

Seri affluence…*José Astorga*…Documented
as the first Seri woodcarver and entrepreneur,
José is called "the rich one." He is said to
possess the land as far as the eye can see and
to have flown to the moon.

Seri modesty...*Victoria*
...Victoria is the sister of José Astorga
and wife of Miguel Barnett.

A Seri gentleman...*Miguel Barnett*
...A woodcarver and a fisherman,
Miguel maintains the appearance
and manner of Seri tradition.

Seri portrait…*Lupe Comito.*

Seri portrait...*Antonio Burgos.*

Seri portrait...*María Luisa*.

Seri elder...*Chico Romero*. Old and blind, Chico carried a cup for handouts. A respected leader, hunter, and fisherman, he negotiated with the Mexicans and other foreigners.

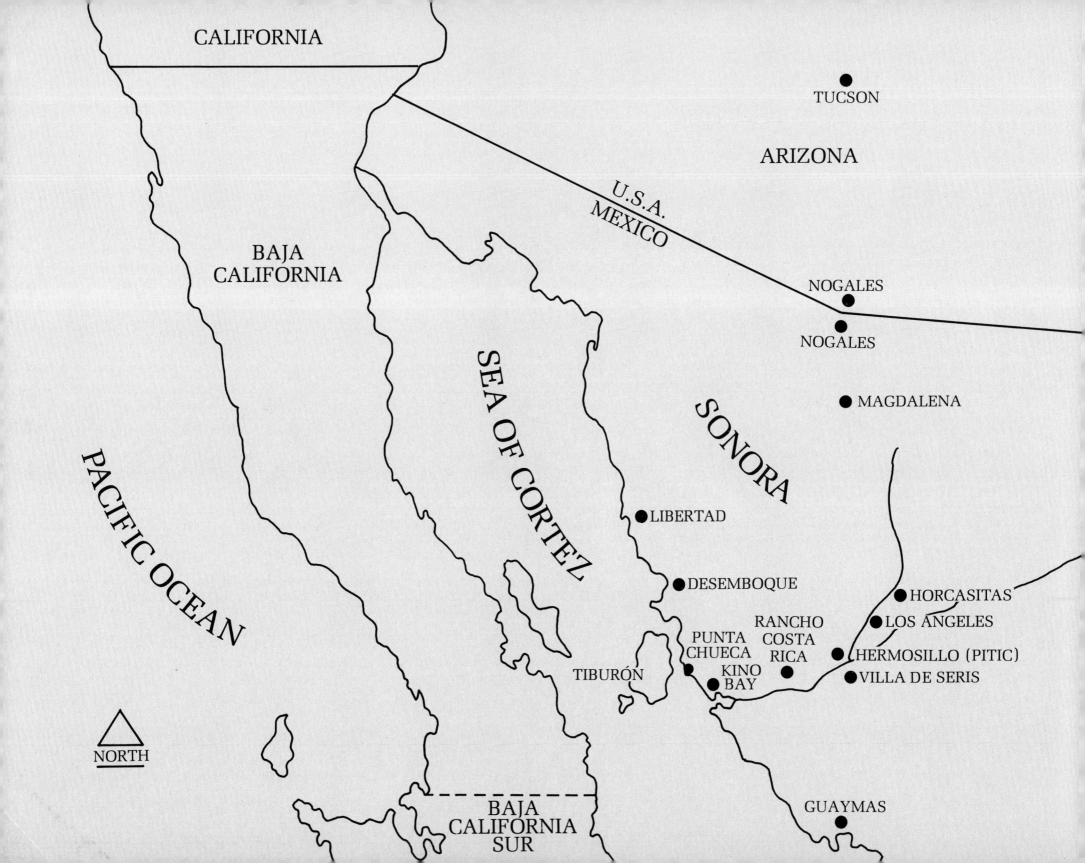

Seriland
—the Seris once claimed this entire area.
The shaded area shows their
present-day homeland.

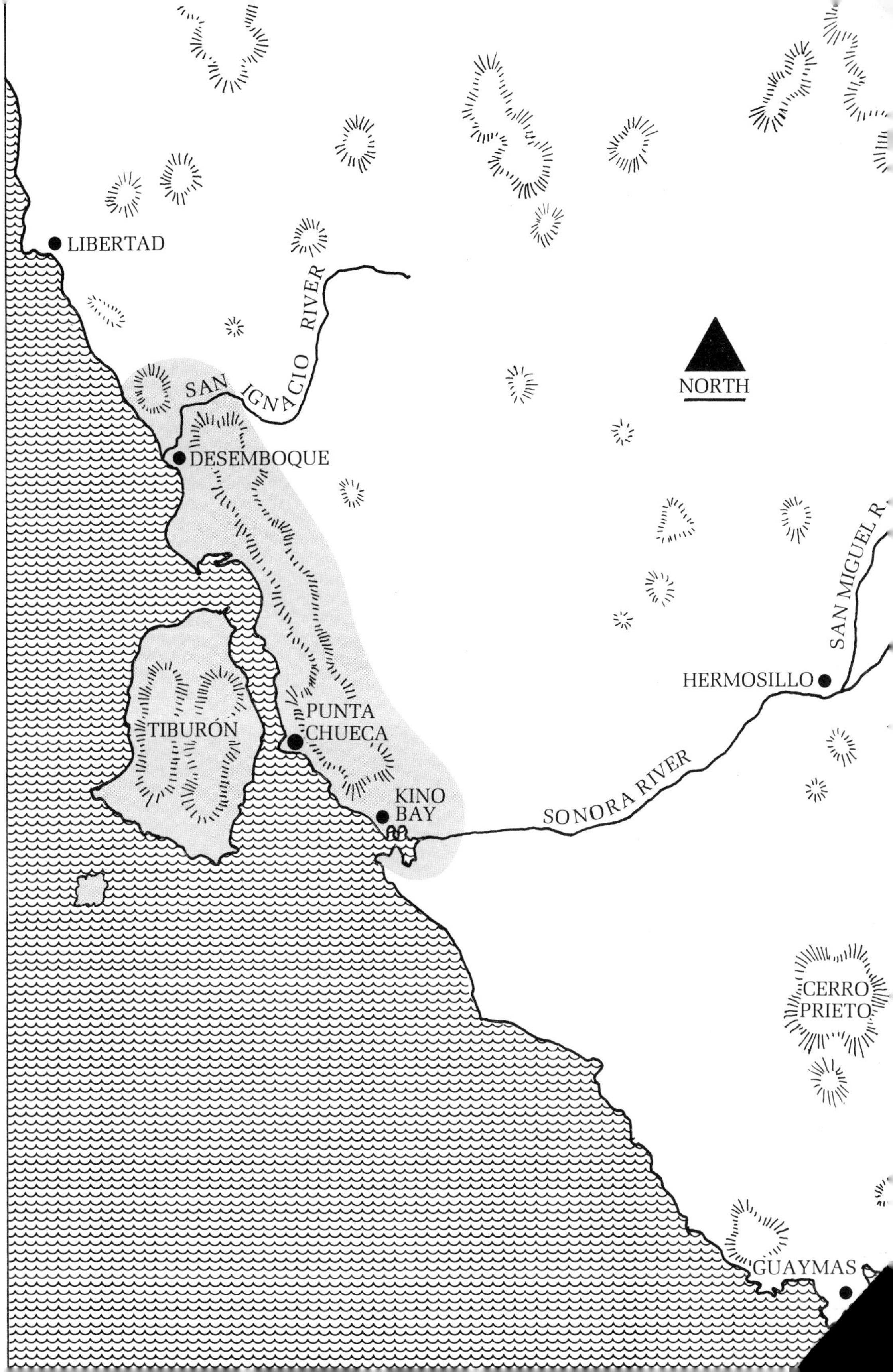

Sonora, Mexico
—home of the Seri Indians.

● LIBERTAD

SAN IGNACIO RIVER

NORTH

● DESEMBOQUE

SAN MIGUEL R.

HERMOSILLO ●

TIBURÓN

PUNTA
CHUECA ●

KINO
BAY ●

SONORA RIVER

CERRO
PRIETO

●GUAYMAS
●

during Audubon's travels in Florida. Audubon had heard "wonderful accounts" of a nearby spring, and Rees graciously took him there. "After breakfast, our amiable host showed us the way to the celebrated spring," Audubon later wrote, "the sight of which afforded me pleasure sufficient to counterbalance the tediousness of my journey."

The plantation was destroyed during the Second Seminole War in 1839. Later, during the Civil War, Union troops dismantled the sugar mill on the site. In the 1880s, the area around the spring was transformed into a resort where visitors were promised "a fountain of youth impregnated with a deliciously healthy combination of soda and sulphur," according to the website FloridaSprings.org. The name was changed to Ponce de León Springs, and in the 1920s, a fourteen-room hotel featuring private baths was built next to the spring. Named the Ponce de Leon Springs Inn, the hotel featured a dining room, cocktail lounge, dance floor, and other amenities. It was in business into the 1960s.

Located just off U.S. Highway 17, one of the major north-south routes into Florida before the interstate system, De Leon Springs became a major tourist attraction in the 1930s, drawing motorists off the road with a variety of amusements. Visitors could not only swim in the cool spring water but enjoy entertainment by the "Jim Rusing Water Skiing, Boat and Jumping Show," featuring Sunshine Sally, the water-skiing elephant (a second elephant, Queenie, performed on skis at the springs as well). A jungle cruise led visitors past a giant cypress tree and a monkey island. Advertised as "Nature's Cameraland," De Leon Springs also had an alligator pen, an "oriental bridge," and a wishing well.

Today, like some other surviving Florida vintage attractions, De Leon Springs is a state park. Aside from swimming and boating, the main draw is the Old Spanish Sugar Mill Restaurant, which opened in 1961 and features make-your-own pancakes. Each table has a griddle built into it, and servers bring guests batter made from flour ground on-site. Despite a lack of air-conditioning, the place is always packed. It features remnants from the original mill and a re-creation of the original waterwheel.

Right: A vintage brochure shows trams that pulled visitors around the park. *Facing page, left*: This statue of Ponce de León with a beauty queen once stood near the park's entrance. *Top right*: Sunshine Sally, the water-skiing elephant. *Bottom right*: An electric-powered boat takes visitors on a jungle cruise.

SEE **Ponce de Leon Springs**

8 MILES NORTH of DELAND on .... FLORIDA U.S 17

"*Nature's Cameraland*"

AT DeLeon Springs, Florida

Canned Youth

A day without Florida orange juice is like a day without sunshine.

Anthony T. Rossi, Tropicana Products, Inc.

In addition to its "Fountain of Youth" springs, Florida boosters have long linked the Sunshine State to good health in a variety of other ways, especially in the marketing of its top agricultural product, citrus. "Emblazoned on billboards and brochures, the orange was the state's most pervasive symbol, bringing together visions of health, sunshine and fertility," writes historian Gary Mormino.

Citrus in Florida traces its roots back to sixteenth-century Spain, land of Ponce de León. Europeans brought the fruit to the New World; in Florida it flourished and evolved into a multibillion-dollar industry. Orlando's Dr. Philip Phillips, who came to Florida in 1894, became one of the state's largest growers and a pioneer in citrus marketing. In the days before frozen orange juice was developed, Phillips linked oranges and good health in the marketing of his canned juice with the slogan, "Drink Dr. Phillips orange juice because the Doc says it's good for you." That message became ingrained in America's psyche.

TOUCH UP YOUR HEALTH
first thing every morning!

FIGHT FATIGUE!

GUARD AGAINST COLDS!

FORTIFY WITH VITAMIN C!

For good health and good looks there's nothing like a daily tonic of wake-up Florida grapefruit, with that zestful, tangy goodness you'll find in no other grapefruit.

Both the fresh fruit and the canned juice are full of natural vitamin C, other vitamins, minerals, and fruit-sugar energy.

At least once a day make it a point to give yourself a tune-up with Florida grapefruit – either the delicious fresh fruit or the equally healthful canned juice.

FLORIDA CITRUS COMMISSION, LAKELAND, FLORIDA

Keep Good Health Tuned Up!

Eat Florida grapefruit, and drink its delicious juice every day!

FROM NATURE'S TREASURE CHEST OF HEALTH AND SUNSHINE

FLORIDA GRAPEFRUIT

FRESH ...OR *CANNED JUICE*

We have a natural skin freshener
that works better inside than outside.

If you're really careful about your skin, you're probably using a "natural" skin freshener, maybe even one that contains extracts of citrus fruit. But all the fruit you put on your face won't do you the amount of good that getting them into your blood stream will. Because your skin can't digest them.

Beauty is more than skin deep. It's the workings of that marvelous machine called your body that digests and extracts from the fruit the vitamins and nutrients that it needs. And it does this better than all the cosmeticians in the world.

One of the things you need for healthy tissue and skin is vitamin C. And since your body can't store it or make it, scientists recommend a daily supply of vitamin C. Oranges and grapefruit are a prime natural source. Grapefruit is especially good to help you shape up because it gives you nutrients without a lot of calories. Oranges, besides being rich in vitamin C and potassium, contain vitamin B, provitamin A and lesser amounts of iron, magnesium and phosphorous. And they both have the fantastically fresh, lively taste of citrus.

You can eat grapefruit and oranges from Florida by their whole, round, delicious selves, or use your imagination to mix them with other fruits, sherbet, or whatever you like. (Try some frozen orange concentrate over yogurt, or grapefruit slices with mashed sweet potatoes!) Even easier, drink grapefruit and orange juice on the rocks or as a spritzer (mixed with soda water).

Florida Citrus Growers
Copyright, State of Fla. Dept. of Citrus, 1973.

Advertising touts the various health benefits of Florida citrus, from "retarding old age" and "fighting fatigue" to a "full measure of health" and "healthy tissue and skin."

PONCE DE LEON DISCOVERED THE REAL "FOUNTAIN OF YOUTH" IN THE TROPICAL FRUITS OF FLORIDA

972 FAMOUS GREEN BENCHES, ST. PETERSBURG, FLORIDA

A Second Life in the Sunshine State: Florida's Silver Revolution

My parents didn't want to move to Florida, but they turned sixty and that's the law.

Jerry Seinfeld

Beginning in the late nineteenth century, folks started coming to Florida in winter in search of relief from their ailments and from the cold northern winters. Some stayed in motels; others purchased vacation homes. But especially after World War II, as the lure of a healthy lifestyle in Florida entered the national consciousness, senior citizens in record numbers began to seek homes in the sunshine year-round. Today the state is abundant with retirement communities and whole cities for retirees. The massive Villages development in central Florida that sprawls across three counties is only the latest major lifestyle settlement for seniors. One of the earliest locales for retirees was the Osceola County city of St. Cloud, promoted as a "soldiers' colony" for Union Civil War veterans in 1909. Fast forward to the 1970s, when William Levitt, inventor of the modern suburb with his postwar creation of Levittown, New York, built the central Florida retirement community of Williamsburg. The same pattern played out all over the state from Sun City Center to Miami Beach.

Clichés have grown up around the influx of the over-sixty set into Florida, from mobile home parks with plastic flamingoes to shuffleboard courts filled with slow-moving seniors. The city of St. Petersburg, long associated with green benches full of retirees, has recently reinvented itself, and now the shuffleboard courts are used by hipsters young and old, as if the whole city had drunk from the fountain of youth.

Right: A 1965 ad for Fort Lauderdale proclaims that "Staying youthful isn't a matter of finding a mystical fountain of youth to grow in . . . it's finding the place where fun and new interests feed the inner springs of life."

Left: Senior citizens in the Sunshine State: Filling water bottles at St. Petersburg's Fountain of Youth, visiting St. Augustine's Fountain of Youth, and sitting on the famous green benches of St. Petersburg.

Florida's gray wave—part of a series of connected and unconnected migrations—occurred in a blink of time.

Gary Mormino, Land of Sunshine, State of Dreams

Why people grow young in Fort Lauderdale

Swimming Pool, Sulphur Springs, Tampa, Fla.

⇻ 4 ⇺

Swimming Holes to Sinkholes: Turning Crystal Waters into Liquid Gold

The State of Water

While the bright sunlight flecks the silvery rocks below with rays of dazzling brightness, an azure tinge encircles every object and surrounds it with a halo of purplish light. It is not strange that they should be deemed to possess a renovating elixir, and to promise, to those who would dwell by their banks and disport in their waters, a restoration of youthful vigor and energy.

George Rainsford Fairbanks,
History of Florida

Surrounded by water on three sides, the state of Florida also has more than seven hundred springs—"the largest concentration of springs on the planet," as journalist Cynthia Barnett has written. It is estimated that more than a quadrillion gallons of water flow underground in the limestone caverns beneath the surface of the state. Throughout Florida's history, the promoters of these artesian jewels—including Warm Mineral Springs and De Leon Springs—often made claims that their spring was the place sought by Ponce de León. Today many of Florida's springs are public spaces, state and local parks used for recreation by millions of residents and visitors every year. Yet the continued stress of overdevelopment, ironically by individuals pursuing the myth of Florida, puts the future of these magical watering holes at risk. The endangered list includes Florida's revered Silver Springs, where the wonder of the crystal clear water has drawn visitors since the steamboat days of Florida tourism.

Right: Illustration from an article titled "The Great Springs of Florida" in *Ford Times* magazine, 1947. *Below*: A mermaid at Weeki Wachee State Park.

Facing page: *Florida Spring* by Florida artist Joy Postle.

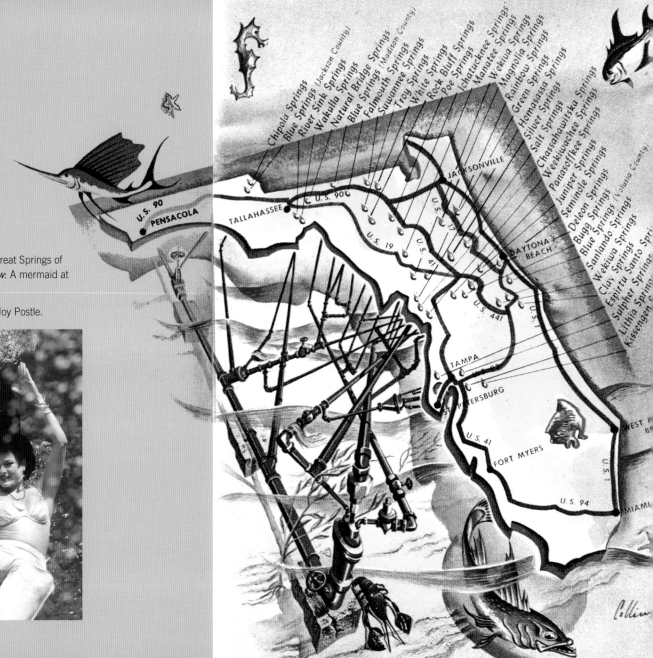

SILVER SPRINGS: NATURE'S UNDERWATER FAIRYLAND

Visitors began arriving at Silver Springs en masse via stagecoach after the Civil War. Steamboats from the St. Johns River navigated the narrow Ocklawaha River to bring the likes of Ulysses S. Grant, Mary Todd Lincoln, and Thomas Edison to the natural phenomenon that photographer Stanley Morrow dubbed "the greatest curiosity in Florida" in the 1880s. The glass-bottom boat, an icon of Florida tourism, was invented at Silver Springs in 1878, according to the attraction's online history, when an enterprising man named Hullam Jones outfitted his dugout canoe with a glass viewing box to expose the wonders underneath. Others say it was Silver Springs resident Phillip Morell who added a glass window to the bottom of his rowboat, forever changing the way in which visitors viewed the waters of the springs.

Above: Early glass-bottom boats were propelled by oars and muscle. *Right*: A bathing-suit-clad beauty adorning the front of a Florida map offers just one example of the inventive marketing blitz created by Silver Springs operators.

Facing page: Gold-dust-like fish food falls from the hands of underwater beauties amid a rainbow of colorful fish.

Newt "The Human Fish" Perry (*top left*); "Underwater Photography 101" in a Bruce Mozert image (*bottom left*); brochure for Ross Allen's Reptile Institute (*center*); map showing the many attractions at Silver Springs (*right*). *Facing page*: A surreal underwater image by Bruce Mozert.

At its peak, Silver Springs spawned a collection of side attractions including Tommy Bartlett's Deer Ranch, Ross Allen's Reptile Institute, the Prince of Peace Memorial, and the Carriage Cavalcade, a collection of horse-drawn vehicles and classic cars.

But the main attraction was always the crystal-clear waters of the springs, where Ocala photographer Bruce Mozert created classic underwater scenes that were used to promote the springs—and Florida—worldwide in the 1950s and 1960s. Scenes supposedly from ordinary life, shot underwater, helped embellish the notion that Florida was a mythic place where the surreal was commonplace.

The springs became a magnet for underwater photos and moving pictures thanks in part to a barrel-chested young Ocala man named Newt Perry, who helped pioneer underwater swimming techniques there in the 1920s and 1930s. Dubbed "The Human Fish" by producer Grantland Rice, Perry invented many of the underwater routines that became standards at other Florida spring attractions, and went on to a legendary career in Florida tourism and underwater cinematography.

As if the incredible natural wonders of the watery world were not enough, promoters created their own fables to embellish the

Left: One of the stops on the glass-bottom boat tours was the Bridal Chamber, the site of a legend about ill-fated lovers whose final resting place was the bottom of the spring.

Above: Visitors crowd a glass-bottom boat, probably in the 1950s.

THE *Legend* OF THE
Bridal Chamber
AT FLORIDA'S SILVER SPRINGS

THE *Legend* OF THE
Bridal Chamber
AT FLORIDA'S SILVER SPRINGS

Above and right: The Seminole Village was added to Silver Springs in 1935 as part of herpetologist Ross Allen's Reptile Institute. Silver Springs was home to indigenous peoples and the Seminole Indians for thousands of years.

histories of the springs. The "Bridal Chamber Legend" was a widely promoted story with a Romeo and Juliet plot told for many years at the attraction by an aged African American storyteller named Aunt Silla. The story ends tragically with both lovers dead at the bottom of the spring. According to a Silver Springs brochure, the rocks of the spring "opened up to receive these unhappy lovers to the bosom of Mother Earth, then closed again over their dead bodies; and people do say their bones still repose there."

The fantastic world of Silver Springs also included a Seminole Indian Village. A 1940s promotional brochure reads: "After your boat trip don't fail to see the Silver Springs Seminole Indian Village. . . . Very interesting—primitive—educational . . . America's

strangest community." The brochure copy went on to declare that "tourists who visit this unique and primitive community are fascinated by these strange Americans who seem to come from the Medieval Pages of History." Treated like a commodity much like the conquistadors treated the New World, the once-feared Seminoles, descendants of Creek Indians and escaped slaves, became an exotic attraction at Silver Springs and other tourist locales including Musa Isle and Tropical Hobbyland in South Florida.

During the era of Jim Crow segregation in Florida, the sights of Silver Springs were made accessible to African Americans at a separate attraction called Paradise Park, which closed during the 1960s. "Nothing like it in the world is what you'll say about Paradise Park,

YOU'LL ENJOY FEEDING THOUSANDS OF FISH!

LOOKING THRU GLASS INTO 80 FEET OF WATER!

PLENTY OF PICNIC TABLES, FREE.

PARADISE PARK SUITS THEM PERFECTLY!

See **FLORIDA'S**
SILVER SPRINGS
FROM
PARADISE PARK
FOR COLORED PEOPLE ONLY

See **FLORIDA'S**
SILVER SPRINGS
FROM
PARADISE PARK
FOR COLORED PEOPLE ONLY

ENJOY WORLD'S MOST FASCINATING GLASS BOTTOMED BOAT RIDE
OVER THE CRYSTAL CLEAR WATERS OF SILVER SPRINGS

the newest and most unusual recreation area now open in Florida for the exclusive use of colored people of America and the world!" exclaims a promotional brochure for the park.

The brochure also states that "Silver Springs probably has the largest flow of any spring in the world, namely, 22,134,780 gallons per hour."

In 1993 the property the attraction occupies was sold to the State of Florida, and today a private company manages the theme park under a long-term lease. Electric glass-bottom boats still glide over the springs, and animal attractions entertain audiences on land. But despite being designated as an Outstanding Florida Water by the state, Silver Springs is in trouble. Its flow and water quality are severely impaired. The amount of water flowing from the springs has declined by 50 percent since 1965. And increased nutrient loading has adversely affected the springs' legendary water clarity.

Left: The second line of the Paradise Park brochure reads: "Opened on Emancipation Day 1949, Paradise Park is regarded by prominent civic, business, and religious leaders thruout the nation as the finest thing of its kind ever built for members of their race."
Above: Increased nitrates have led to an increase in algae growth in Silver Springs.
Right: Silver Springs' iconic horseshoe palm still survives today with a little support.

WEEKI WACHEE: SPRING OF LIVE MERMAIDS

Perhaps no spring better represents the idea of Florida as a fantasyland than the mermaid-filled waters of Weeki Wachee. The Hernando County spring became an attraction in the late 1940s when Newt Perry teamed with Walton Hall Smith and leased the property surrounding the then-obscure spring from the city of St. Petersburg.

Perry, who refined his underwater theatrics first at Silver Springs and then Wakulla Springs, trained young women in swimming techniques, including the art of taking breaths of air from a submerged hose. His original mermaids, including local teenagers and synchronized swimmers from St. Petersburg, performed in an underwater theater in which visitors gazed at them through large windows. He was a brilliant marketer and created photogenic stunts for the mermaids such as drinking sodas underwater and the famed adagio pose, in which one mermaid lifted another over her head. Perry was "just doing what people had done for thousands of years—putting the spin on an age-old myth," Lu Vickers notes in *Weeki Wachee: City of Mermaids*.

In 1948 Hollywood took advantage of the crystal-clear waters of Weeki Wachee. The movie *Mr. Peabody and the Mermaid*,

Top: Newt Perry carries Nancy Tribble to a water tank in Tampa as part of the promotion for the 1948 movie *Mr. Peabody and the Mermaid*. *Above, left*: Dramatic underwater images promoted Weeki Wachee.

Facing page: In 1959, Weeki Wachee built a new, larger underwater theater.

filmed at the springs, offered a huge publicity opportunity for the attraction, and the mermaid tail worn by the film's female star, Ann Blyth, inspired the standard costume for the spring's underwater performers.

The water was so clear in the early days of the attraction that audiences had trouble believing the mermaids were actually underwater, not part of an elaborate hoax. Vickers suggests that, "in the late 1940s and early 1950s, watching girls perform for thirty or forty minutes seemingly underwater was as exciting and surreal as watching Neil Armstrong step onto the moon in the 1960s." At the end of 1950s, a new, expanded underwater theater was constructed, and the attraction was sold to ABC-Paramount, resulting in celebrity appearances and more elaborate story lines for the mermaid shows.

Today Weeki Wachee is a state park, and the mermaids continue the tradition of performing before appreciative fans.

Top left: A vintage brochure from the period in which ABC Television owned Weeki Wachee features celebrity endorsements. *Bottom left*: A contemporary mermaid. *Bottom right*: Vintage postcard titled "Poetry in Motion."

Facing page: Double exposure of mermaids, taken from the underwater theater, 1952.

VIEWING OF FISH FROM THE
UNDERWATER GALLERY.
NATURE'S GIANT FISHBOWL,
HOMOSASSA SPRINGS, FLORIDA.

HOMOSASSA SPRINGS
SPRING OF 10,000 FISH

"Nature's Best Kept Secret"

WALK UNDER WATER

U.S.19 75 Mi. N. of Tampa—St. Petersburg, Fla.

DON'T MISS...
HOMOSASSA
...SPRINGS
NATURE'S OWN ATTRACTION
FLA.

OTHER SPRINGS ATTRACTIONS

Homosassa Springs in Citrus County was developed by an avid sportsman named David Newell who was attracted by the rare mix of saltwater and freshwater fish present in the spring. He dubbed it "Nature's Giant Fishbowl" when he opened it in 1940 and created a unique underwater viewing gallery, a version of which still offers great views of aquatic life today.

After Newell, subsequent owners re-named the attraction Homosassa Springs and used an image of an Indian maiden on their advertising—a nod to the Indian-sounding name. (According to a State of Florida website, "Homosassa" is a Creek word meaning "place of many pepper plants.")

This page, right: Contemporary view through the underwater observation area at Homosassa Springs.

Bottom, right: Vintage postcard featuring Indian maiden signage used by the Citrus County attraction.

Left: Homosassa Springs touted its natural assets with an underwater observatory allowing one to "walk under water."

Facing page: An early observatory featured signs to help with fish identification.

Like nearby Silver Springs, Rainbow Springs in Marion County once had glass-bottom boats, as well as underwater "submarine" boats, a steamboat, and an odd leaf-shaped monorail. But after Interstate 75 funneled tourists farther east to Walt Disney World, Rainbow went out of business. Like Wakulla and Weeki Wachee, both Homosassa and Rainbow Springs are open today as Florida state parks.

Above and right: Rainbow Springs' unique "Photo-submarine" boats allowed for viewing of "unusual colorful underwater beauty."

Facing page: Vintage postcard featuring bathing-suit-clad beauties at Rainbow Springs.

07—Sun Deck, Boat House at Famous Rainbow Springs, Florida

Beauty Above and Below, Silver Springs, Florida

O-119—Sanlando Springs Tropical Park, Orlando, Fla.

The Future of Florida's Fountain of Youth

Ponce de León opened the floodgates to Florida, and a half millennium later, the Land of Flowers is full to the brim. In 2012, Florida ranked as the fourth-largest state in the nation in terms of population, and many experts say the natural resources of this earthly paradise surrounded by water are stretched to the point of collapse. The source of most of Florida's drinking water and the springs that dot the state, the Floridan aquifer, is in danger of being stretched beyond capacity, and much of the recharge zone, where water seeps into the earth to refill the aquifer, is paved over.

How Floridians resolve the challenges of growth related to water might very well determine whether the charms of this beautiful land and the lifestyle symbolized by the pursuit of eternal youth are passed on to the next generation.

In Florida there is summer in winter. Healing waters pour from rock-bound fountainheads to add to man's span of life. Through an atmosphere without smoke, dirt, or grime the sun sends its priceless ultraviolet rays to build and to cure. Florida is a place for rejuvenating rest to the weary and ill, a place where children grow strong, and a nation recreates.

Kim's Guide to Florida

Above: A sign at Wekiva Springs State Park is the perfect metaphor for the future of ecosystems of springs statewide. *Facing page, left*: Warm Mineral Springs is owned by the City of North Port and operated by an outside vendor as a spa. *Middle*: Silver Springs, now owned by the State of Florida but leased to an outside vendor, faces the strain of increased development. *Right*: Weeki Wachee State Park, where the Southwest Florida Water Management District must balance maintaining this vintage attraction and the needs of development around this once-rural spring.

> **Water has, indeed, defined most of our state's history and culture and influenced the intricate interplay between our natural and human-made environments. It will also shape our future.**
>
> **Francine Cary, Forum magazine**

WATER: FLORIDA'S MOST PRECIOUS RESOURCE

Juan Ponce de León was the first-known European to set foot on Florida's beaches, making him the state's original tourist, as historian Tracy Revels notes. Ponce explored both the Atlantic and Gulf coasts, and we may never know for sure whether or not he actually ventured inland to one of Florida's springs. Archaeological evidence has shown that for centuries before Ponce ever got there, Native Americans had lived along Florida's beaches, rivers, lakes, and springs. In the eighteenth and nineteenth centuries, as pioneering souls began to settle in the state, being near clean water was critical, and settlements arose around good water sources.

Soon Florida's promoters and developers presented this state of magical waters as "something unlike any other, a tropical wilderness where travelers might be renewed and reinvented," according to Revels.

Above: Tubers float down the springs run at Rock Springs in Orange County.

Facing page, left: A vintage advertisement invites readers to "join us in swimming, in fishing—in all the other sports and health and fun that Florida offers." *Right*: An ad from 1958 invites the viewer to "soak up some health . . . swim in Florida waters.

You are invited, too!

Join us for a real vacation — in Florida — this spring! Skip the uncertain weather. Join us in this land of sunshine at its very loveliest. Join us in swimming, in fishing—and in all the other sports and health and fun that Florida offers you. Plan days of sightseeing. You'll discover a world of interesting things to see and do all over Florida. You'll go home feeling like a million dollars, rested and refreshed as never before!

this is FLORIDA

INDIAN RIVER REGION—Typical family scene, repeated again and again at the many secluded and uncrowded beaches found in this section.

Come, soak up some health... swim in Florida waters!

You'll feel wonderful, yet spend no more than ordinary vacations cost

The welcome mat is out all over Florida and fun and health are yours for the taking.

Slip into buoyant salty surf along Florida's sun-drenched shores and feel your mood brighten —your spirits soar. Relax on warm, friendly sands and toast tensions away.

Kindly, beneficial waters are everywhere. In inland Florida, crystal-clear lakes and springs provide the finest bathing, boating, water sports and fishing you'll find anywhere.

You'll see vivid subtropic nature, too. Orchids that grow wild, towering palms, thousands of brilliantly colored flowers—fragrant citrus groves,

exotic tropical jungles and lush green shrubs.

Go boating or skiing — or if it's big-game thrillers you're after, you'll find 'em all—tarpon, sail, dolphin and dozens of others—down either coast for miles and miles. And do you know, no point in the state is more than 60 miles from ocean or Gulf!

There is no pleasanter way to rejuvenate than "toning" up in Florida. For all its benefits, you need spend no more than on an ordinary vacation. Now, and all summer through, rates in the most deluxe hotels and motels imaginable, are low as just modest facilities elsewhere.

Florida
YEAR ROUND LAND OF GOOD LIVING

GULF STREAM COAST—Swimming pools that dot this sun-kissed wonderland plus miles of sandy beaches make the southeast coast unsurpassed for bathing.

WEST COAST — Dad makes like a skin diver while family enjoys a boat ride in blue Gulf of Mexico. This area also features snow-white sand beaches.

CENTRAL FLORIDA—Aquatic star performing in crystal-clear spring near Ocala. Among other exciting spectacles are rodeos and famous citrus groves.

NORTH FLORIDA—Both here, and in Central Florida, transparent springs and lakes with glistening white sand beaches are perfect for family vacation fun.

FREE! NEW 100-PAGE FLORIDA VACATION GUIDE Most complete Florida guide ever available. Information packed. 143 color illustrations. Maps. Tells what to see, do—all over Florida. MAIL COUPON NOW!

State of Florida • Room 1702-H
Commission Building, Tallahassee, Florida
Please send new 100-page Florida Vacation Guide.

Name _____

Address _____

City _____ Zone ____ State ____

EXECUTIVES: For full factual story on Florida industrial advantages, write: Development Commission, Dept. T, on your business letterhead.

Living on a peninsula with abundant bays, rivers, and lakes, we Floridians should set the standard for the nation in thinking deeply about our relation to water.

Ron L. Cooper

To serve those travelers, railroad tycoons built elaborate resorts along both coasts, and steamboats ventured into the wilderness on rivers fed by springs. Soon wooden hotels were built to give health seekers a place to stay when visiting the healing waters of the state's springs.

Over time, roadside attractions also popped up at some of the state's more famous springs, and, eventually, after the interstate highway system caused the roadside traffic to diminish, a few became state parks. Clever marketers helped promote all the waters of Florida as a source of perpetual health and vitality. Even citrus grown in Florida could ward off disease and was a necessary ingredient of a healthful lifestyle. As Americans lived longer and had the means to retire, communities for senior citizens sprang up near the water, so that older folks could have the Fountain of Youth within their grasp. For five centuries, the idea of Florida has been linked to the life-giving properties of its water, both real and mythic.

In the twenty-first century, it's quickly becoming apparent that Florida's liquid gold, its water, is more precious than ever. The development of interior portions of the state is catching up to that of coastline communities, and the effect of millions of new residents has been profound on Florida's water. As Cynthia Barnett puts it: "A century ago, Floridians thought their biggest problem was too much water where people wanted to settle. . . . Now, our biggest problem is that we do not have enough water where people want to settle."

Both quantity and quality of the water are at issue. In addition to tapping the underwater aquifer to its limit, the fertilizer dumped on Floridians' lawns and used by agriculture has had a detrimental effect on the state's water, increasing levels of nitrates that encourage the growth of algae. The sandy bottoms of Florida's springs are becoming covered with fuzzy slime, and the once clear spring water is turning green in parts of the state. Some springs are at risk of drying up, repeating a process that has occurred before. And sinkholes are becoming an issue in places where such a large volume of water is pumped from the underground aquifer that the land actually collapses.

Left: A swimmer in Central Florida's Wekiva Springs.

Facing page, bottom left: A no-swimming sign at Volusia County's Green Springs, water formerly promoted to have restorative powers. *Top left*: A billboard near Silver Springs advertises legal assistance for sinkhole victims. *Right*: Wekiva Springs.

WHITE SPRINGS AND KISSENGEN SPRINGS: GONE BUT NOT FORGOTTEN

The stories of White Springs on the Suwannee River and Kissengen Springs in central Florida show what can happen to the magical waters that Floridians long assumed would bubble from the ground forever. These two springs, once well used and vital, both dried up in the twentieth century.

The water at White Springs, or White Sulphur Springs, was said to have curative powers that could bring "relief from rheumatism, kidney trouble, nervousness, and other ailments," according a website for the Town of White Springs.

In the late 1880s, owners of the land surrounding the springs built a four-story structure around the healing waters, and a resort town including fourteen luxury hotels emerged from the Florida woods. Today the norm inside the thick concrete walls that were once the base of the four-story building is a puddle of mucky green water. The flow of the water appears initially to have been adversely affected by nearby phosphate mining. When the mines' demand for water diminished over time, increased pumping from the aquifer in northern Florida and southern Georgia contributed to the springs' demise, according to some authorities.

Above: The Spring House in 1919, from the Suwannee River. *Facing page*: Inside the Spring House, 1919. Well-known visitors included Henry Ford and Teddy Roosevelt.

Phosphate mining was undoubtedly the cause of the demise of Polk County's Kissengen Springs. Originally named Spring De Leon, it offered patrons amenities including bathhouses "of the most modern style," according to an 1883 issue of the *Bartow-Informant* newspaper.

The story goes that after a visitor compared the Polk springs to the medicinal waters at Bad Kissingen in Germany, its name was changed to capitalize on the fame of the European spa town. Spa owners built a wooden dam to create a circular pool, slowing the flow of the spring waters to the nearby Peace River. A favorite of Polk residents for seventy years, Kissengen Springs had a pavilion with a dance floor, a pool table, and large picnic grounds where political rallies were held.

As early as 1898, however, a study by the U.S. Geological Survey had determined that the springs' flow of 20 million gallons a day could be useful for something other than recreation. "Great volumes of water like some of the large springs of Florida are especially valuable to manufacturing industries which need pure water," wrote Prof. B. M. Hall, who studied the springs' potential. That potential was never met, because Kissengen Springs dried up in the winter of 1950, leaving only a "pool of stagnant water," according to a 1950 newspaper article. Another article that revisited the spring's history ran with the headline "The Spring That People Killed."

Facing page: An undated photograph shows early facilities at the spring. *Immediate left*: A recently erected historical marker, ironically placed in a park whose land was donated by a phosphate mining company, honors the spring. *Left*: A newspaper ad lists the features of "Polk County's Favorite Pleasure Resort."

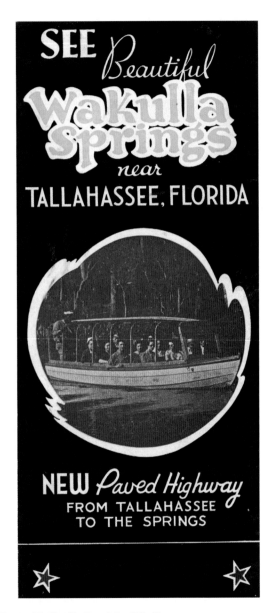

SEE *Beautiful*
Wakulla Springs
near
TALLAHASSEE, FLORIDA

NEW *Paved Highway*
FROM TALLAHASSEE
TO THE SPRINGS

Wakulla Springs
LAND OF ROMANCE
AND MYSTERY

WAKULLA SPRINGS—WORLD'S LARGEST AND DEEPEST SPRINGS JUST SOUTH OF TALLAHASSEE FLA.

SPRINGS: AN UNCLEAR FUTURE

While some springs have vanished, others offer examples of diminished water quality. Two examples, popular for generations of Floridians, are Wakulla Springs near Tallahassee and Sanlando Springs, in Seminole County between Sanford and Orlando. Both once were privately owned attractions with amenities such as diving platforms and restaurants.

One of the largest springs in Florida, Wakulla was once owned by Alfred du Pont's brother-in-law and financial manager, Ed Ball (1888–1981), a towering figure in Florida business and politics who may very well have been the most powerful man in the state. He built the Wakulla Springs Lodge in 1937 and developed the springs into an attraction with glass-bottom boats, a lodge, and a dining room. According to historians, there is little evidence that Ponce de León was in the vicinity of this spring near Tallahassee, yet Ball claimed that the Spanish explorer was fatally wounded there and said he had the arrowhead to prove it.

Newt Perry developed underwater swimming techniques there, in what is one of the largest and deepest freshwater springs in the world—perhaps *the* largest. The crystal-clear spring water was also home to movie production, including World War II training

films, *Tarzan* and *Creature from the Black Lagoon* features, and even the filming of an underwater disaster movie, which involved submerging a portion of a jumbo jet in the springs.

Wakulla Springs even had an underwater mascot named "Henry the Pole-Vaulting Fish," a black bass that would "vault" itself across a submerged pole to the delight of an audience in the glass-bottom boats.

Water-clarity issues go back to the mid-twentieth century, according to Tracy Revels in her book *Watery Eden: A History of Wakulla Springs*. A 2005 report on the springs' hydrology notes that native aquatic plant species have been replaced by invasive hydrilla and algae and describes "an increase in the frequency of dark-water days, during which the water in the basin is too dark to permit the glass-bottom boats to operate." Despite the water-quality issues, the site remains a popular state park.

This page: A contemporary shot of Wakulla Springs. *Facing page, far left*: Vintage brochure touts the "new paved highway from Tallahassee to the Springs." *Right*: Promotional materials put forward the claim that Ponce de León perished at the spring.

Sanlando Springs, however, remains off-limits to the public. Central Floridians began utilizing the springs for recreation in the 1880s, when it was called Hoosier Springs, according to historian Jim Robison, and generations enjoyed swimming, picnicking, and dancing there. A developer named Frank Haithcox dammed the spring to create the swimming areas in 1926 and renamed it Sanlando because of its location between Sanford and Orlando. Between about 1950 and 1970, Sanlando's swimming pool, giant water slide, and beautifully landscaped gardens made it one of the area's most popular spots in the summer.

A history on the development's website concludes: "To the disappointment of many but to the good fortune of those lucky enough to have lived or will live in The Springs Community, Sanlando Tropical Park was acquired and privatized by Mr. Earl Downs in 1970. Mr. Downs transformed The Park into what has become known as simply 'The Springs.'"

In 2004, a report on the Wekiva springshed, of which Sanlando Springs is a part, concluded that "water resources of the area are being negatively impacted by man's activities as related to nitrogen contamination." In 2011, the St. Johns Water Management District, alarmed at the spring's diminished flow, asked local utilities to reduce the amount of water they pumped from around the spring in an attempt to restore it to previous levels. Today the future of Sanlando Springs' health remains cloudy.

Top: Vintage postcard shows the addition of walls around the swimming area, colorful landscaping, and a diving board. *Bottom*: Contemporary image of the spring within the gated development.

Left and above: Vintage brochure for Sanlando Springs. *Below*: Early view of Sanlando Springs before it was developed into a "Tropical Park" in the 1950s.

FINDING THE FOUNTAIN OF YOUTH TODAY

It has been said that one of the challenges facing Florida today is that, while the bodies of transplanted residents are here, their hearts are elsewhere—in the states "up north" where they grew up. The future of what was once considered paradise and its magical waters may well be determined by how deeply today's Floridians embrace their adopted state and become involved in preserving the special places that make the state unique. There are still amazing sites that many folks have not discovered.

Here's a list of some you may wish to explore on your own.

Above: Central Floridians enjoy Rock Springs near Apopka. *Top right*: An aqua-aerobics class at Warm Mineral Springs in North Port. *Bottom right*: This well in Punta Gorda was touted by early-twentieth-century promoters as the Fountain of Youth. *Far right*: Entrance to the Fountain of Youth attraction in St. Augustine.

Fabulous Florida

DISCOVER YOUR OWN FOUNTAIN OF YOUTH!

SPRINGS/PARKS

1. De Leon Springs State Park, De Leon Springs
2. Edward Ball Wakulla Springs State Park, Wakulla Springs
3. Ellie Schiller Homosassa Springs Wildlife State Park, Homosassa
4. Fountain of Youth Park, St. Petersburg
5. Juan Ponce de León Landing, Melbourne
6. Rainbow Springs State Park, Dunnellon
7. Silver Springs, Silver Springs
8. Weeki Wachee Springs State Park, Weeki Wachee

HISTORIC SITES

9. Flagler College, St. Augustine
10. Fountain of Youth Archaeological Park, St. Augustine
11. Nature and Heritage Tourism Center, White Springs
12. Spring Park, Green Cove Springs

SPA/HEALTH RESORTS

13. Safety Harbor Spa and Resort, Safety Harbor
14. Warm Mineral Springs, North Port

TO A FLORIDA SPRING

How shall I name the blue that swells
From out thy subterranean wells—
The hue unnameable that sleeps
Within thy vast and Stygian deeps?

Through endless corridors of night
Thou seekest for the blessed light—
Till thou hast found the secret way
That leads thee to the dome of day.

Imprisoned in thy restless stream,
Ten thousand orient sapphires gleam.
Thy darting denizens are drest
In sunglint from the peacock's breast.

The mastodon once came to drink
At thy primeval chasm's brink,
And ghosts of Eden's vanished flowers
Still bloom in thy subaqueous bowers.

Turquoise and jade, thy rippled sands,
O'erlaid with rainbow's dancing bands—
And fragile webs of amber lace
'Round violet-shadowed wells of space.
　　　　　　　　　　—*Joy Postle*

Ponce De Leon Springs Syndicate

ACKNOWLEDGMENTS

The journey that led to this book began with my adventure partner and wife, Julie. I thank her for allowing me the space to work on this project and for not judging me for spending our money on postcards and ephemera. The book wouldn't have happened without the mentorship and encouragement of my good friend Joy Wallace Dickinson, a fantastic writer who does more than she realizes to keep Florida history alive. Thanks also to my family for their support, loaned images, and eBay gift cards. I am appreciative of Lu Merritt and Margaret Ross Tolbert for helping to raise my awareness of the plight of Florida springs. A big shout out, too, to John Moran and Leslie Gamble for seeing the potential of this project and connecting me to the folks who could make it a reality. And finally I'd like to acknowledge fellow University Press of Florida authors Lu Vickers, Tim Hollis, and Gary Monroe for their work highlighting Florida's mid-twentieth-century past, a colorful era of mermaids, glass-bottom boats, and bubbling springs.

BIBLIOGRAPHY

Anderson, Damann L. "A Review of Nitrogen Loading and Treatment Performance Recommendations for Onsite Wastewater Treatment Systems in the Wekiva Study Area." Report for Hazen and Sawyer, P.C., February 2006.

Audubon, John James. "Third Florida Episode: Spring Garden." In *Life of John James Audubon, the Naturalist, Edited by His Widow.* New York: G. P. Putnam, 1870.

Bair, Cinnamon. "Polk Chronicles: Kissengen Spring Was Spot for Fun." *Lakeland Ledger,* August 23, 2011. www.theledger.com.

Barclay, Shelly. "Accounts of and Searches for the Fountain of Youth." http://historicmysteries.com.

Barnett, Cynthia. *Blue Revolution: Unmaking America's Water Crisis.* Boston: Beacon Press, 2011.

———. "Hope Lives, Even as Marker Notes Polk's Kissengen Springs, Dry since 1950." *Tampa Bay Times,* September 25, 2011.

———. *Mirage: Florida and the Vanishing Water of the Eastern U.S.* Ann Arbor: University of Michigan Press, 2008.

———. "Toward a Water Ethic." *Tampa Bay Times,* June 5, 2011.

Bartram, William. *Travels of William Bartram.* Edited by Mark Van Doren. New York: Dover, 1955.

Braden, Susan R. *The Architecture of Leisure: The Florida Resort Hotels of Henry Flagler and Henry Plant.* Gainesville: University Press of Florida, 2002.

Branson, Seth. "A Tale of Three Henrys." In "Florida Theme Issue," edited by Beth Dunlop, special issue, *Journal of Decorative and Propaganda Arts,* no. 23 (2002).

Burt, Al. "An Essay on Florida Springs." http://apalacheehills.comsprings/Springbook/Quotes.htm.

Clark, James C. "Fountain of Myths: The Legends That Have Sprung up around Ponce De Leon's 'Discovery' Have Kept Florida's Oldest Attraction Forever Young." *Orlando Sentinel,* January 6, 1992. www.chicago tribune.com.

Copeland, Leeila S., and J. E. Dovell. *La Florida: Its Land and People.* Austin, Texas: Steck, 1957.

De Herrera y Tordesillas, Antonio. "Historia general." In "Early Visions of Florida." www.earlyfloridalit.net.

Deese, A. Wynette. *St. Petersburg: A Visual History.* Charleston, S.C.: History Press, 2006.

"DeLeon (or Ponce De Leon) Springs." http://apalachee hills.comsprings/DeLeon.htm.

"De Leon Springs State Park." www.floridastateparks. org/deleonsprings/.

Drye, Willie. "Fountain of Youth—Just Wishful Thinking?" *National Geographic.* http://science.nationalgeographic .com science/archaeology/fountain-of-youth/.

Dunlop, Beth. "Inventing Antiquity: The Art and Craft of Mediterranean Revival Architecture." In "Florida Theme Issue," edited by Dunlop, special issue, *Journal of Decorative and Propaganda Arts,* no. 23 (2002).

"E. H. Tomlinson." *St. Petersburg Evening Independent,* December 8, 1938. http://bayart.weebly.comfountain-of-youth-pier.html.

Federal Writers' Project. *WPA Guide to Florida: The Federal Writers' Project Guide to 1930s Florida Written and Compiled by the Federal Writers' Project of the Works Progress Administration for the State of Florida.* 1939. Reprint. New York: Pantheon, 1984.

"Florida Springs history." www.dep.state.fl.us/springs/ about.htm.

Forum: The Magazine of the Florida Humanities Council (Fall 2001, Summer 2002, Winter 2005, and Fall 2011).

"Fountain of Youth, Punta Gorda, Florida." www.way marking.com.

Francis, J. Michael. "Who Started the Myth of a Fountain of Youth?" In "Viva Florida!," special issue, *Forum:*

Above: Promotional photo for Warm Mineral Springs. *Facing page*: Mermaids at Weeki Wachee Springs State Park carry on the tradition of underwater performance begun by the attraction's founder, Newt Perry.

The Magazine of the Florida Humanities Council (Fall 2011).

Fraser, Walter B. *The First Landing Place of Juan Ponce de Leon on the North American Continent in the Year 1513*. St. Augustine: Fountain of Youth Archaeological Park, 1956.

Fuson, Robert H. *Juan Ponce de León and the Spanish Discovery of Puerto Rico and Florida*. Granville, Ohio: McDonald and Woodward, 2000.

Gannon, Michael. *Florida: A Short History of Florida*. Rev. ed. Gainesville: University Press of Florida, 2003.

———, ed. *The New History of Florida*. Gainesville: University Press of Florida, 1996.

———. *Michael Gannon's History of Florida in 40 Minutes*. Gainesville: University Press of Florida, 2007.

Gotschall, Phil, and Fred Allen. *Healing Waters: A History of De Leon Springs*. Pamphlet available at the De Leon Springs State Park gift shop, 2005.

Hartzell, Scott Taylor. "Edwin H. Tomlinson: St. Petersburg's Greatest Benefactor." In *Remembering St. Petersburg, Florida: Sunshine City Stories*, vol. 1. Charleston, S.C.: History Press, 2006.

Hatton, Hap. *Tropical Splendor: An Architectural History of Florida*. New York: Knopf, 1987.

"History of White Springs." http://whitesprings.org/www. whitesprings.org/history.htm.

Hoffman, Susan E. "The Mystery of Warm Mineral Springs." *Charlotte Sun-Herald*, November 28, 2006. www.suncoasteam.comarticles/55.html.

Hollis, Tim. *Glass-Bottom Boats & Mermaid Tails: Florida's Tourist Springs*. Mechanicsburg, Penn.: Stackpole, 2006.

———. *Selling the Sunshine State: A Celebration of Florida Tourism Advertising*. Gainesville: University Press of Florida, 2008.

"Juan Ponce de Leon and the Spanish Discovery of Puerto Rico." Marker in Juan Ponce de Leon Park, Melbourne, Fla.

Keegan, William F. "Columbus, Hero or Heel?" *Vista*, March 24, 1991. www.flmnh.ufl.edu/caribarch/columbus.htm.

Kimball, Ethel Byrum, ed. *Kim's Guide to Florida*. Anna Maria, Fla.: Kim's Guide, 1950.

Martin, Greg. "Kissengen Spring among the Lost Resources." *Charlotte Sun-Herald,* May 18, 2008. http://itech.fgcu.edu/faculty/ndemers/mining/kissengen%20 Springs%20may%2008.htm.

Milanich, Jerald T. "Original Inhabitants." In *The New History of Florida,* edited by Michael Gannon. Gainesville: University Press of Florida, 1996.

Missall, John, and Mary Lou Missall, eds. *In Their Own Words: Selected Seminole "Talks."* Dade City, Fla.: Seminole War Foundation, 2009. (Contains Coacoochee's speech about the afterlife and his dream.)

Moncada, Carlos. "'Fountain of Youth' Memories Bubble in Bay." *Tampa Tribune*, January 5, 2008. Tampa Bay Online. www2.tbo.com.

Monroe, Gary. *Silver Springs: The Underwater Photography of Bruce Mozert*. Gainesville: University Press of Florida, 2008.

Mormino, Gary R. *Land of Sunshine, State of Dreams: A Social History of Modern Florida*. Gainesville: University Press of Florida, 2005.

———. "Gary Mormino Speaks about Florida's 2013 Quincentennial." YouTube video. Florida Humanities Council Scholar Summit, October 30, 2009.

Peck, Douglas T. "Misconceptions and Myths Related to the Fountain of Youth and Juan Ponce de Leon's 1513 Exploration Voyage." New World Explorers, Inc. www.newworldexplorersinc.org/FountainofYouth.pdf.

Prizer, Edward L. "Winter Wilds: Central Florida's Tourism Industry Started with Steamboat Adventures along the St. Johns River." *Legacy: A People's History of Central Florida,* a publication of *Orlando Magazine*, 2000.

"Quotes about Florida Springs, a Bit of Poetry, an Al Burt

Florida Seminole Indians and their Dug-Out Canoe

Essay, and Springs in the Bible." http://apalacheehills.comsprings/Springbook/Quotes.htm.

Revels, Tracy J. *Sunshine Paradise: A History of Florida Tourism.* Gainesville: University Press of Florida, 2011.

———. *Watery Eden: A History of Wakulla Springs.* Tallahassee, Fla.: Sentry Press, 2002.

Rothchild, John. *Up for Grabs: A Trip through Time and Space in the Sunshine State.* New York: Viking Penguin, 1985. 2nd ed., Gainesville: University of Florida Press, 2000.

Sculle, Keith A. "The Promotional Efficacy of Brochures, Booklets, and Picture Postcards for the Fountain of Youth, St. Augustine, Florida." *Transactions* (Pioneer American Society) 29, (2006).

Silver Springs. "General History" and "Historical Timeline." www.silversprings.comheritage.html.

Sitler, Nevin, and James Parrish. "Quick Facts," "Fountain of Youth." For the St. Petersburg Museum of History. http://downtownstpete.ilovetheburg.comarticle/Where-is-Tony-Today/3178.

Spear, Kevin. "Water District Steps up to Push to Save Orlando-area Springs, lakes." *Orlando Sentinel,* July 28, 2011.

"St. Petersburg Began as a City with Many Piers." http://bayart.weebly.com.

Stamm, Doug. *The Springs of Florida: A Natural History Field Guide for Divers, Snorkelers, Paddlers, and Visitors to Florida's Legendary Springs.* 2nd ed. Sarasota, Fla.: Pineapple Press, 2008.

Ste. Claire, Dana. "Dana Ste. Claire Speaks about Florida's 2013 Quincentennial." YouTube video. Florida Humanities Council Scholar Summit, October 30, 2009.

Stowe, Harriet Beecher. 1873. *Palmetto Leaves.* Reprint, Gainesville: University Press of Florida, 1999.

Tolbert, Margaret Ross, ed. *AQUIFERious.* Gainesville, Fla., 2010.

Vickers, Lu. *Cypress Gardens, America's Tropical Wonderland: How Dick Pope Invented Florida.* Gainesville: University Press of Florida, 2010.

———. *Weeki Wachee, City of Mermaids: A History of One of Florida's Oldest Roadside Attractions.* Gainesville: University Press of Florida, 2007

www.warmmineralsprings.com.

Wynne, Nick, and Richard Moorhead. *Paradise for Sale: Florida's Booms and Busts.* Charleston, S.C.: History Press, 2010.

IMAGE CREDITS

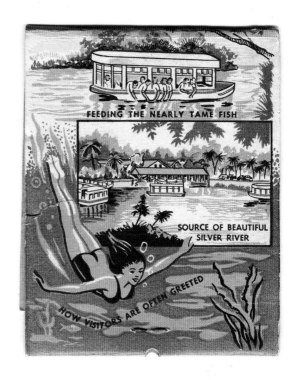

The Fountain of Youth, St. Augustine, Florida

FOUNTAIN OF YOUTH

...ING WAS DISCOVERED IN

RECORDED A LANDMARK

WIREPHOTO

The Fountain of Youth

IMMORTALIZED BY JUAN PONCE DE LEON

ST. AUGUSTINE, FLORIDA

WARM Mineral SPRINGS
VENICE, FLORIDA

THE REAL Fountain of Youth

The FOUNTAIN of YOUTH

Memorial Park and Gardens

Immortalized by Juan Ponce de Leon

ST. AUGUSTINE, FLA.

Rick Kilby is a graphic designer living in Orlando, Florida, and president of Kilby Creative.

The University Press of Florida is the scholarly publishing agency for the State University System of Florida, comprising Florida A&M University, Florida Atlantic University, Florida Gulf Coast University, Florida International University, Florida State University, New College of Florida, University of Central Florida, University of Florida, University of North Florida, University of South Florida, and University of West Florida.

FROM NATURE'S
TREASURE CHEST
OF HEALTH AND
SUNSHINE

VIVA FLORIDA 500
1513-2013

In April 1513, Juan Ponce de León arrived on Florida's east coast. He led the first European exploration of southern North America and is responsible for naming the peninsula *La Florida*.

While our state's geologic history is approximately 700 million years old and its material history dates back more than 12,000 years to the American Indians who first lived here, the Spanish arrival in *La Florida* marked a new era. The peoples and cultures that came together under Florida's first flag laid the groundwork for what would eventually become the United States. Under the French, British, Confederate, and American flags that followed, Florida became home to many: Protestant Huguenots and Jewish Americans, Black Seminoles and WWII veterans, mermaids and martyrs of the Civil Rights movement.

Beginning in 2013, celebrations like Viva Florida 500 will commemorate the arrival of Ponce de León in *La Florida* and recognize the many diverse cultures that comprise our state and impact its rich history, including the fiftieth anniversary of Civil Rights legislation in 2014 and, in 2015, the 450th anniversary of the founding of St. Augustine, the oldest continuously occupied European-established city in the continental United States.

Joining in the celebration of these significant milestones and honoring the people, places, and unique history of our state, the University Press of Florida is pleased to designate the Florida history and culture titles published in 2013–2015, including *Finding the Fountain of Youth: Ponce de León and Florida's Magical Waters*, as Florida Quincentennial Books.